Pip and Pop

Written by Natasha Paul

Illustrated by Erin Brown

Collins

Kim picks the kit.

Pip tips the sack.

Pip can pat it.

Pop can tap it.

Kim pops it in.

Kim pops the cap.

Pop can dip it.

Pip pops the cap.

It is on the cat!

Pop packs the sack.

Pip picks a man.

/c/

14

k

ck

15

🐾 Review: After reading 🐾

Use your assessment from hearing the children read to choose any GPCs, words or tricky words that need additional practice.

Read 1: Decoding

- Remind the children that two letters can make one sound. On page 2, point to **picks** and ask the children to sound out and blend the word (*p/i/ck/s*). Ask: Which two letters make the /c/ sound? (*ck*) Can they find the same sound but spelt differently on this page? (*K/i/m, k/i/t*)
- On page 4, ask them to find the /c/ sound. How is it spelt? (*c/a/n, c*)
- Look at the "I spy sounds" pages (14–15). Point to the kettle on page 14 and then the "k" at the top of the page and say: I spy a "k" in kettle. Challenge the children to point to and name different things they can see containing the /c/ sound. (e.g. *sink, fork, cutlery, cake, case, curtain, cucumber, cupboard, sock, duck, building blocks, socket*) You could ask the children about spellings, e.g. Ask: How is the /c/ in that word spelt?

Read 2: Prosody

- Choose two double page spreads and model reading with expression to the children.
- Ask the children to have a go at reading the same pages with expression.

Read 3: Comprehension

- For every question ask the children how they know the answer. Ask:
    - On pages 2 and 3, who empties the sack? (*Pip*)
    - On page 4 and 5, who is making the gingerbread shape? Which word tells you this? (e.g. *Pop*; *tap*)
    - On pages 10 and 11, do you think the cat got in a mess by mistake? How? (*Yes*, e.g. *Pip squeezed the tube of icing and it shot onto the cat*)
    - On pages 12 and 13, which word tells us that Pop is putting things away into a sack? (*packs*)